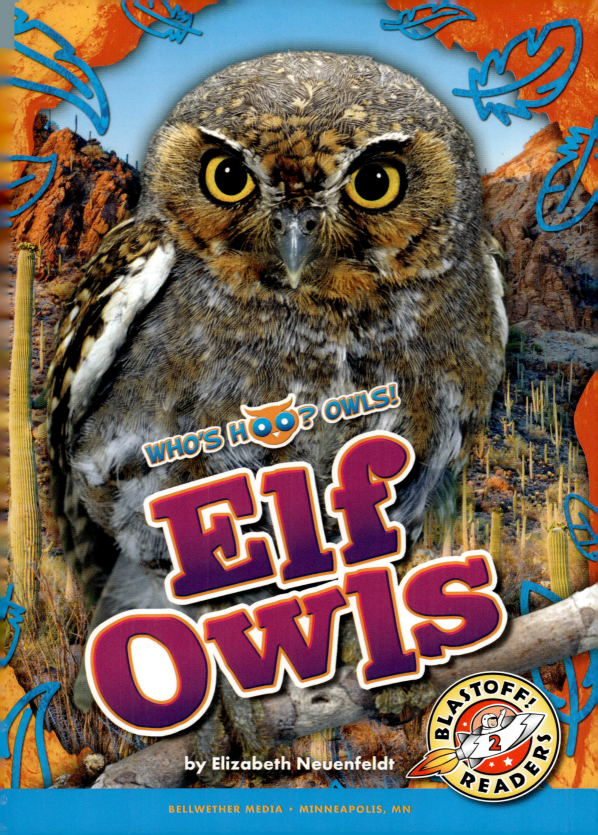

WHO'S HOO? OWLS!

Elf Owls

by Elizabeth Neuenfeldt

BLASTOFF! READERS

BELLWETHER MEDIA • MINNEAPOLIS, MN

Blastoff! Readers are carefully developed by literacy experts to build reading stamina and move students toward fluency by combining standards-based content with developmentally appropriate text.

LEVELS

Level 1 provides the most support through repetition of high-frequency words, light text, predictable sentence patterns, and strong visual support.

Level 2 offers early readers a bit more challenge through varied sentences, increased text load, and text-supportive special features.

Level 3 advances early-fluent readers toward fluency through increased text load, less reliance on photos, advancing concepts, longer sentences, and more complex special features.

★ Blastoff! Universe

Reading Level

Grade K → Grades 1–3 → Grade 4

This edition first published in 2024 by Bellwether Media, Inc.

No part of this publication may be reproduced in whole or in part without written permission of the publisher. For information regarding permission, write to Bellwether Media, Inc., Attention: Permissions Department, 6012 Blue Circle Drive, Minnetonka, MN 55343.

Library of Congress Cataloging-in-Publication Data

Names: Neuenfeldt, Elizabeth, author.
Title: Elf owls / by Elizabeth Neuenfeldt.
Description: Minneapolis, MN : Bellwether Media, Inc., 2024. | Series: Blastoff! Readers. Who's hoo? Owls! | Includes bibliographical references and index. | Audience: Ages 5-8 | Audience: Grades 2-3 | Summary: "Relevant images match informative text in this introduction to elf owls. Intended for students in kindergarten through third grade"-- Provided by publisher.
Identifiers: LCCN 2023008918 (print) | LCCN 2023008919 (ebook) | ISBN 9798886874143 (library binding) | ISBN 9798886876024 (ebook)
Subjects: LCSH: Elf owl.
Classification: LCC QL696.S83 N48 2024 (print) | LCC QL696.S83 (ebook) | DDC 598.9/7--dc23/eng/20230309
LC record available at https://lccn.loc.gov/2023008918
LC ebook record available at https://lccn.loc.gov/2023008919

Text copyright © 2024 by Bellwether Media, Inc. BLASTOFF! READERS and associated logos are trademarks and/or registered trademarks of Bellwether Media, Inc.

Editor: Rebecca Sabelko   Designer: Brittany McIntosh

Printed in the United States of America, North Mankato, MN.

Table of Contents

World's Smallest Owls	4
Insect Eaters	12
Life of an Elf Owl	18
Glossary	22
To Learn More	23
Index	24

World's Smallest Owls

Elf owls live in **deserts** and dry forests throughout North America.

They are the smallest owls in the world!

Elf owls only grow up to 5.5 inches (14 centimeters) tall.

They have small wings. Each wing is around 5 inches (13 centimeters) long.

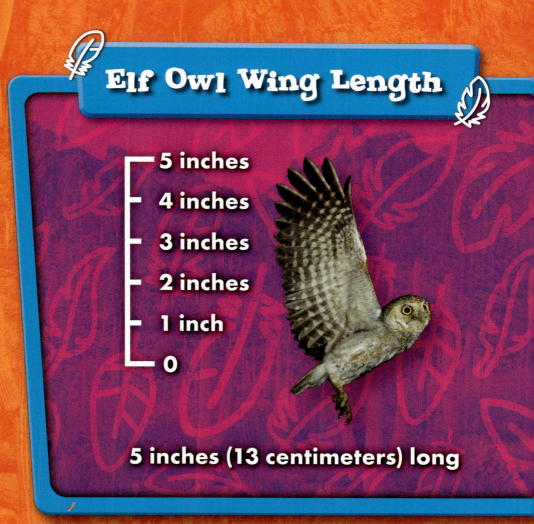

Elf Owl Wing Length

- 5 inches
- 4 inches
- 3 inches
- 2 inches
- 1 inch
- 0

5 inches (13 centimeters) long

Elf owls have big, round heads. White feathers above their big, yellow eyes look like eyebrows!

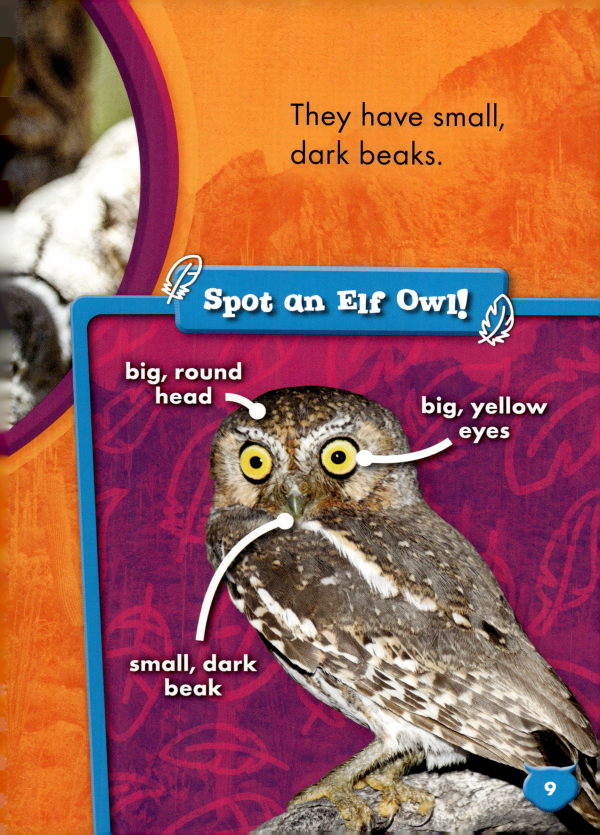

They have small, dark beaks.

Spot an Elf Owl!

big, round head

big, yellow eyes

small, dark beak

Elf owls have brown, gray, and white feathers with light spots.

Their tails are short. They have sharp **talons**.

Insect Eaters

Elf owls hunt at night. But desert nights become cool in winter. There are fewer **insects**.

The owls **migrate** to find more food.

Elf Owl Food

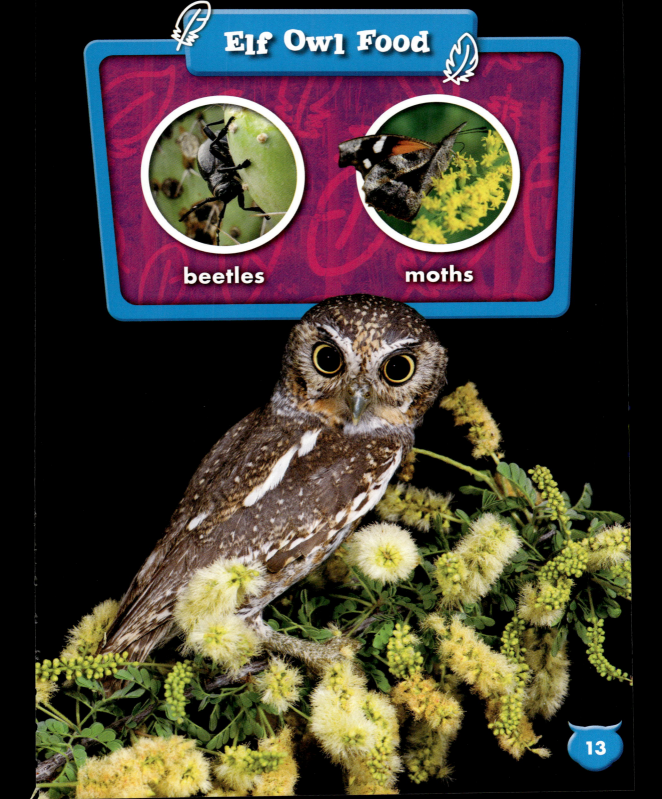

beetles   moths

insect

Elf owls hunt in the air and on the ground. They use their excellent hearing to find insects.

They catch food with their beaks and talons.

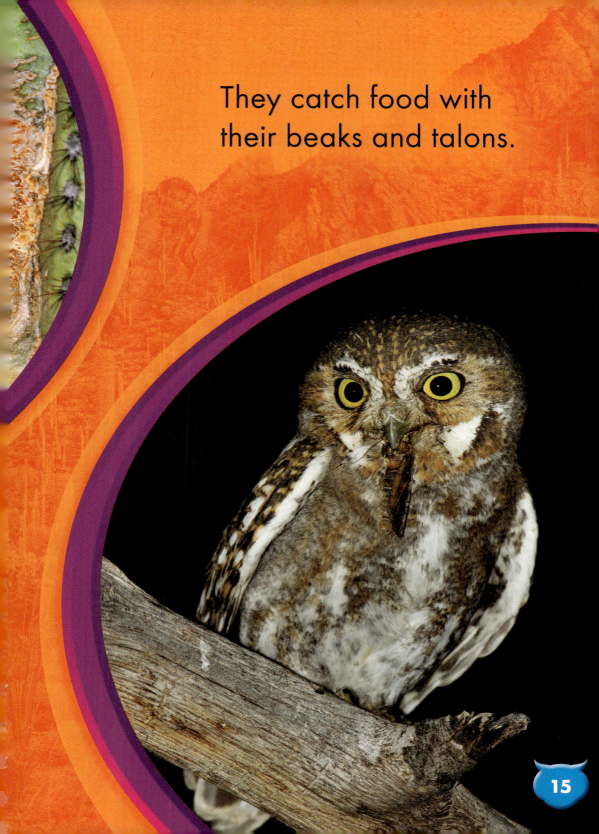

These small owls must look out for snakes and other **predators**.

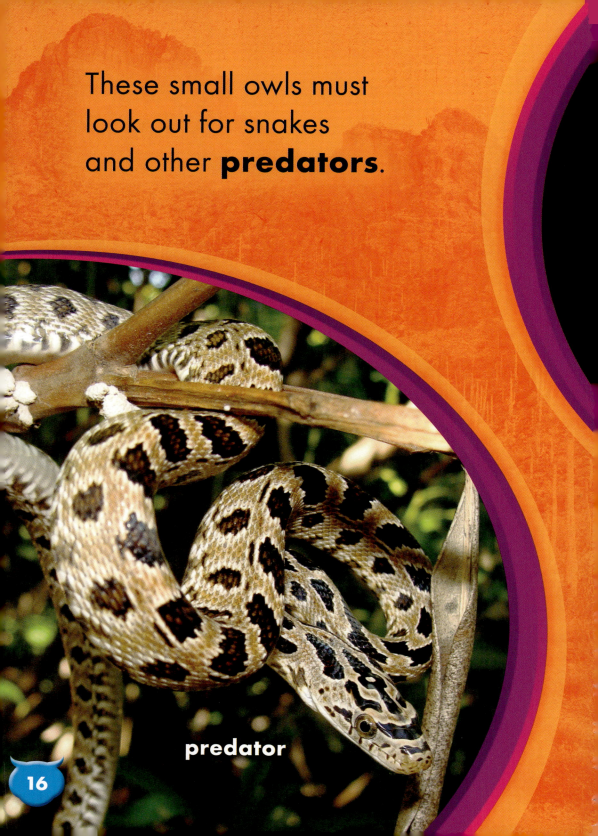

predator

Sometimes elf owls attack enemies that come too close!

Life of an Elf Owl

Elf owls mostly live in pairs. They **roost** together in **cavities** in trees and cactuses.

Females also lay eggs in the cavities.

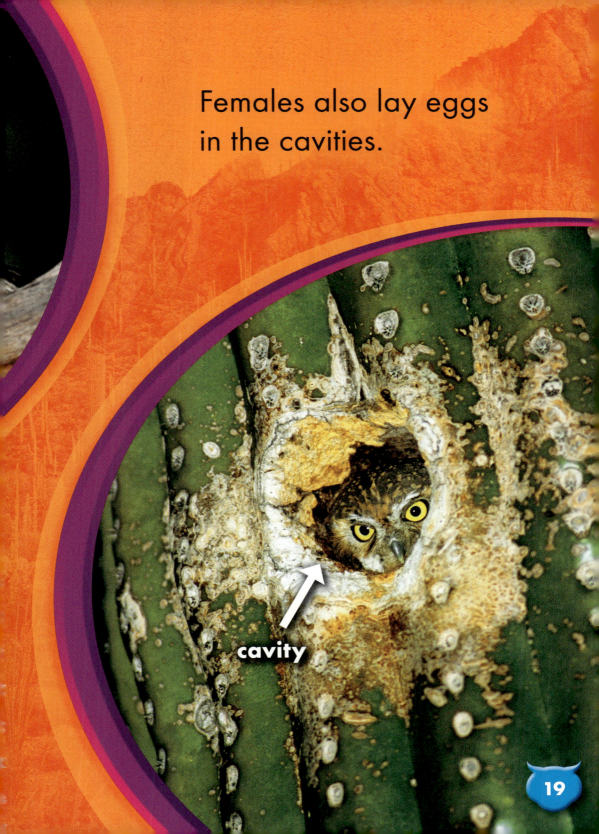

cavity

Female elf owls lay up to five eggs. **Owlets** will **hatch** after 24 days.

Owlets become **fledglings** about one month later. Soon they are all grown up!

owlets

Glossary

cavities—holes or spaces inside of things; elf owls use cavities for roosting and nesting.

deserts—dry lands with few trees and little rainfall

fledglings—young owls that have feathers for flight

hatch—to break out of an egg

insects—small animals with six legs and hard outer bodies; an insect's body is divided into three parts.

migrate—to travel with the seasons

owlets—baby owls

predators—animals that hunt other animals for food

roost—to rest or sleep

talons—the strong, sharp claws of owls and other raptors

To Learn More

AT THE LIBRARY

Barnes, Rachael. *Burrowing Owls*. Minneapolis, Minn.: Bellwether Media, 2024.

Clausen-Grace, Nicki. *Owls*. Mankato, Minn.: Black Rabbit Books, 2019.

Porter, Jane. *So You Want to Be an Owl*. Somerville, Mass.: Candlewick Press, 2021.

ON THE WEB

FACTSURFER

Factsurfer.com gives you a safe, fun way to find more information.

1. Go to www.factsurfer.com.

2. Enter "elf owls" into the search box and click 🔍.

3. Select your book cover to see a list of related content.

Index

attack, 17
beaks, 9, 15
cavities, 18, 19
colors, 8, 9, 10
deserts, 4, 12
eggs, 19, 20
eyes, 8, 9
feathers, 8, 10
females, 19, 20
fledglings, 20
food, 12, 13, 14, 15
forests, 4
growing up, 21
hatch, 20
heads, 8, 9
hearing, 14
hunt, 12, 14
migrate, 12

night, 12
North America, 4
owlets, 20
pairs, 18
predators, 16
range, 4, 5
roost, 18
size, 5, 6, 7, 8, 9, 11, 16
spots, 10
tails, 11
talons, 11, 15
wings, 7
winter, 12

The images in this book are reproduced through the courtesy of: Anthony Mercieca/ Dembinsky Photo Associates/ Alamy, front cover, p. 23; All Canada Photos/ Alamy, pp. 3, 19; Rick & Nora Bowers/ Alamy, pp. 4, 7, 12-13, 14, 17, 21 (top left, top middle); Susan E. Viera, pp. 6, 8; AZ Outdoor Photography, p. 9; Suzanne Renfrow, p. 10; Glenn Bartley/ All Canada Photos, p. 11; Charles Melton/ Alamy, pp. 12, 20, 21 (top right); Charles T. Peden, p. 13 (top left); Conrad Barrington, p. 13 (top right); Jared Hobbs/ All Canada Photos, p. 15; Matt Jeppson, p. 16; Ed Schneider, p. 18; Urbach, James, pp. 20-21.